I0098030

Copyright © 2006/2012 by Almetia Mack

Published in the United States of America by
         Power through Faith Publishing
         P.O. Box 20581
         Greensboro, NC 27420

         ISBN 978-0-9707320-6-4

         Amack336@aol.com

♥ *Dedication*♥

I would like to dedicate this book to the Holy Spirit who guided me through every chapter. When I thought it was all over He brought all things to my remembrance.

I would also like to dedicate this book to my parents whom I miss very much, the late Mr. Otis & Mrs. Mave Thomas, Gerald & Greg Rush and all the Saints of Seed Planting Christian Church.

Acknowledgements

A special thanks to my loving husband and Pastor, Bobby Mack, who always encourages me. I will never cease to thank God for blessing me with you and our beautiful children and grandchildren. I love you all so very dearly!

To my precious sisters, Mia and Frances, Seed Planting Christian Church, my niece Venita, her son Alexander (Jay) and all the saints of God who have encouraged and prayed for me.

TABLE OF CONTENTS

A   Renewed   Mind

(Ephesians 4:23-24) And be renewed in the spirit   of your mind; (24) And that ye put on the new man,   which after God is created in righteousness and true holiness.

Chapter 1

A Renewed Mind

I remember lying on my bed one evening, just thinking on the Lord and God began to speak a revelation to me. I have different color handkerchiefs that I take to church with me and God began to show me an illustration with those handkerchiefs. The largest one God began to say to me, *"This is you; the smaller ones were things that attached themselves to you while growing up."*

God began to show me these handkerchiefs tied one to another beginning with the larger which represented me, then childhood hurts, rejection, insecurities, low self esteem, abuse and so on. God spoke to me and said, *"This is what a lot of my people are carrying around."*

Then God said, *"Those that have been raped, physically and mentally abused, broken relationships, divorce, sexual sin, fear, hurt in the church, lost of a loved one, those that dealt with alcohol, drugs, pornography, homosexuality, and the list goes on. They give their heart to me and they don't realize their mind must be renewed. This is the only way they can be transformed into that new creature my Son died for them to become."* When God comes into your life and saves you, God makes you free from these things.(John 8:32) ***"And you shall know the truth, and the truth shall make you free."*** The enemy (Satan) then comes to your mind with the memory of that ordeal, and if he can get you to think on this, he can cause you to think that you are still in the same place you were before you got saved.

Remember Satan can only bring the memory to you because he knew you before you gave your heart to God. He knew what made you angry, sad, glad, what turned you on and off, his job is to keep you where he is and that is in the past. Satan knows that he does not have a future and he wants the same for you.

Satan wants you to return to that familiar place.

When you have been locked up for so long, you don't know how to deal with freedom so we go right back to his territory. I saw a program on television one day it was a program about men that had been locked up for 20 to 50 years in prison. After they were set free they did not know how to handle freedom. One man after being locked up for 40 years, was released from prison and he said he could not handle the outside world. He was given a job bagging grocery, he said he could not fit in, so he tried to steal something to go back to prison, finally he hung himself. Satan wants you to return to that familiar place. It may be painful, you may have suffered many things, you may

A Renewed Mind

have been abused, but you return to that place because you have grown comfortable there and no matter how bad it feels you return there because it is a familiar place. People will stay in a church, knowing that they are not getting fed the word of God but, because mother and grandmother went to this church, they stay there, this is a soul tie that binds. A lot of times we do not know how to handle an unfamiliar place. A lot of times it is the change that we fear.

There is an enemy and the moment you receive Christ into your life, you enter into a war that was already in progress (spiritual war). (Ephesians 6:12) For we wrestle (or struggle) not against flesh and blood, but against principalities, against powers, against the rulers of darkness of this world, against spiritual wickedness in high places. I read where we are in a war, battle, and a fight. We are in a personal match or battle with the most cunning, deceitful foe ever created; it is a life and death struggle. That battle is for our soul. God, in His love, is not willing that any should perish, His will is that we follow "Him." Satan on the other hand, wants us to follow him. Therefore, we are in a struggle. At times, it feels like we are being pulled in two different directions at once. At times, it feels like we might be torn apart. But Praise be to God for He has equipped us for every attack of the enemy. (Read Eph. 6:10-17). We have been destined for victory. Your wife, husband, boss neighbor, mother, father, sister or brother is not your enemy, Satan is, and he is the one behind every action that seems to be coming against you.

Now that you know who the enemy is, you must realize you cannot fight him physically; you must fight him in the spirit, with the word of God. (Read Matt. 4:1-11). We must FIGHT SATAN THROUGH THE WORD. When he comes to us we must do like Jesus, tell him, "IT IS WRITTEN.

Alma (I will call her) and I begin to talk and we became good friends. We would go shopping together, out to eat, I noticed she would watch me as I would often tell my husband of the love I have for him, she would dress like me, mimic after me, I soon found out that Alma had been involved in lesbianism. She finally told me one day how she wanted to learn how to do those things women do. She really began to get good at it.

One day we were talking and she began to tell me how some times it felt like she was still there in the same place she use to be. I began to tell her that it was a spirit that wanted his home back. (Matt.12: 43-45) *"When an unclean spirit goes out of a man, he goes through dry places, seeking rest, and finds none. Then he says, "I will return to my house from which I came." And when he comes, he finds it empty, swept, and put in order. Then he goes and takes with him seven other spirits more wicked than himself, and they enter and dwell there, and the last state of that man is worse than the first."* I told her that the enemy was bringing the memory back to get her to start thinking of how it use to be. I also told her that it's like a tooth that has been extracted but once the feeling comes back it seems as if that tooth is still there. God has made you free now you have to be transformed by the renewing of your mind through the word of God.

When you have been involved in something over a period of time the enemy will try to keep you in the past. Satan knows if you dwell on the past it will cause you not to make it to the present, even though you may have given your heart to God, pray, fast and read your bible. Remember your mind is Satan's battleground. Have you ever thought on something so hard that it's almost like you are there or you can taste it? I love chocolate cake and sometimes I can think of that cake and it seems as if I can taste it, well that is exactly how the enemy works. Satan's goal is to have you think on this situation or circumstance so much until you began to taste it, once you can began to taste it, you find yourself going right back to who or whatever it was that had you bound.

Remember your mind is Satan's battleground.

I can remember growing up, we did not have a lot there were days I wondered where we were going to get our next meal from. After I grew up if I mentioned buying a car or a house, this is what my mother would say to me, "*you don't need to get an expensive house or car, buy you a car that's in good enough condition to take and bring you. Make sure you get a house that you can afford to pay for, you don't have to get anything fancy*." This is all I heard from my mother growing up, so I always looked and settled for second hand things. The best was out of the question. I never looked at a brand new car because in my mind I could hear my mother's voice, "*buy you a car that's in good enough condition to take and bring you*." Buying a brand new house was something I always wanted to have but again I could hear her voice.

After I gave my heart to God, I was driving home one day and I wanted to build some rooms onto our mobile home. The Lord had told me earlier that I could have any kind of house I wanted, well because my mind was so use to settling for second best I thought it was really a big deal to get some rooms built on. All of a sudden the Lord begin to speak to me, "*I gave my best so you don't have to settle for second best, he gave his life and it was all for you to have the best. He gave you a better hope, testament, covenant, promises and sacrifices; He not only gave you eternal life, but an abundant life. All these things you have inherited so stop settling and walk in your inheritance.*"

The only way you can be transformed, you must have a renewed mind

One day my mother and I were talking and she began to tell me about her childhood. "*My mother died when I was six months old, my sister was two and my father took my brother and left us with my grandmother,* she said.

A Renewed Mind

I can remember my grandmother a little, my sister and I Stayed with my aunt and she had three children.
We were always moving because we could not afford to pay the rent. I remember times when we would sometimes stay in abandoned houses until someone came along and made us move. My aunt would make us pick cotton and she would take our money. We never got anything for Christmas, her children would always get something for Christmas and my grandmother would tell us Santa Claus had given out of toys before he got here. I can remember getting only one pair of shoes, I was barefoot most of the time," she said, with a sad look in her eye. Then it hit me like a ton of bricks, we never owned a new house we always settled for that too little house to rent, my father bought a new car once but he would not have if he had listened to my mom.

My mother was tied to the things that held her bound while growing up, not wanting to get put out of the house because you can't afford to pay for it. Just get something that you can afford no matter what it looks like so you won't lose it. (Romans 12:2) *"And be not conformed to this world: but be ye transformed by the renewing of your mind, that ye may prove what is that good, and acceptable, and perfect, will of God."* The only way you can be transformed, you must have a renewed mind. If your mind becomes transformed, your action becomes transformed, if your action becomes transformed, your behavior becomes transformed.

1

Silence Is A Root For
Shame & Guilt To Grow

(Isaiah 54:4) Fear not; thou shalt not be ashamed: neither be thou confounded; for thou shalt not be put to shame; for thou shalt forget the shame of thy youth, and shall not remember the reproach of thy widowhood any more.

Chapter 2

Silence Is a Root for Shame & Guilt to Grow

One of Satan strategies is to keep us in silence. **Shhh**…Satan says**, "*Don't tell anyone about that, they will not like you, they will look at you funny, if you tell, they will not love you anymore,*"** and he goes on and on to keep you in silence. A child gets raped or molested and the predator says, "***Don't you say anything about this or I will kill your family, your family won't love you anymore, or no one will believe you, I will say you are lying and who do you think they will believe***?" These are just some of the things the enemy (Satan) uses to keep us in silence. Satan wants you to stay silent because he knows that as long as you don't reveal it, he has a foot hole, he has something he can hold (strong hold) over your head, he likes having a hold card to use against you. The longer you keep silent the more shame and guilt grows, the fact that you don't believe you can talk about it is fertilizer for the shame.

Once you expose it, it loses its Strength

You must address and release these feelings or they will rob you of your joy. Our bodies were made to release, that is why we have eyes, nose, mouth, ears and other areas to release, if we don't release these things we become sick, high blood pressure, stress, it affects us mentally as well as physically. It is the same way in the spirit, we must release, find someone you can trust to talk to. Once you expose it, it loses it strength, for example, Say you did something and someone saw you do it, because you do not want it told they will always hold this thing over your head or may even try to black mail you. ***"If you don't do this or if you don't give me that*, they say, " *I'm telling*."** That's a strong hold they have against you, but once you make up in your mind and say, **"*go ahead and tell whomever because I'm not holding this any longer I'm going to tell it myself*,"** you have just broken that strong hold. This is how Satan wants to hold things over our heads; he knows that as long as we keep silent and never expose it he has a strong hold against us.

I remember when I was three years old; my mother was washing me up, she had sat me on this stool and I did not have any clothes on, someone knocked at the door and she went to answer it. My fathers' friend was in the room with us and when my mother left to go and answer the door, he came over to me and he begin to put his fingers between my legs. I can remember it so well because he had those long fingernails. I remember how bad it hurt, I closed my legs and he began to say to me, **"*Open your legs*"** and before he could open my legs up again my mother came back into the room. I never told anyone about that because I thought people would look at me funny, they would like nor accept me and I dared not tell my parents. I begin to notice how much I disliked older men, I was afraid to be around them.

I remember when I graduated from high school a couple of my friends and I went to Ohio, we were walking from the store one-day and we met these two men that were in service. The guy that I met called me a few times and he began to talk about taking me to New York for the weekend to shop, as we talked I asked him his age. He told me he was 38 years old, (I was 18 at the time), when he told me his age it totally turned me off. *"You are old enough to be my father,"* I replied. That was the end of that relationship. I remember my friends' uncle trying to talk to me it turned my stomach. All this time I just thought I did not like older men, especially men ten years or older than myself.

The longer you keep silent the more shame & guilt grows.

After I gave my heart to God I still held this shame for 20 years, when I finally told my husband what happened to me, it was easy also to talk to my family about it, the burden I carried for years was lifted. I realized I no longer felt the same about older men. I released this shame and guilt I had been holding all those years. I was free; Satan no longer held me in bondage. God is about making us free; Satan is about keeping us in bondage. (Galatians 5:1) *"Stand fast therefore in the liberty wherewith Christ hath made us free, and be not entangled again with the yoke of bondage."* Entangle means ensnare, entrap, to burden by, to be oppressed by, to be subject to, because of its

16

connection to a yoke.

> *Satan loves for us to go into a marriage with secrets and lies.*

e

Teresa (I will call her) begins to say, *"I just can't tell my fiancée about me, if he knew I was raped he will stop loving me, he may even call off the wedding. I love him so much I don't want to lose him."* This is another strategy Satan uses, he loves for you to go into a marriage with secrets and lies, and this is something he can use against you. Many times you have to tell or cover up one lie to tell another one, so this vicious cycle goes on and on. Teresa is going into a marriage in bondage. If she told her fiancée the truth and he stops loving her or calls off the wedding, he never loved her anyway.

Let me tell you the story about Bill and Jill:

Bill met Jill through a friend, Jill was about to graduate from high school and Bill had graduated two years earlier. Jill and Bill began to date and fall in love. They had sex one night and she became pregnant so they got married right after graduation. Jill's parents were divorced when she was only 10 years old; she never forgave her father for leaving her. Jill had been raped when she was 14, afraid it would ruin their relationship she never told Bill.

Silence Is a Root for Shame & Guilt to Grow

Trust had been broken even before they got married. (1 Thess. 4:3) *"For this is the will of God, even your sanctification, that ye should abstain from fornication."* God wants us to flee fornication because he knows that if we are strong enough to say no before we get married, Satan will have a hard time convincing us that our mate is cheating after we get married, when we abstain from sex before we get married. In the back of your mind you will say he/she did not have sex with me I don't believe he/she will have sex with anyone else, why? Because we have a bond. When that bond is broken and you go on and have sex or get caught in lies, in your mind you will think, well they had sex with me, or they lied to me before we got married, they could be having sex with someone else now. Satan now has something he can use in this marriage.

After they were married and the baby was born, if Bill would go anyplace even to the grocery store and stay longer than Jill anticipated, she would began to say to herself**, " He must be with another woman I know he's not at the store this long."   "Anyway, he had sex with me before we got married."** Remember (John 10:10) *"The thief cometh not, but for to steal, and to kill, and to destroy."* He wants to kill your marriage and he has a better chance of doing that if he has something to hold over your head before you get married (It is called a strong hold). Jill became very jealous of her husband; it did not matter what he said she never believed him. They begin to quarrel then it led to physical fighting, Bill was fed up with the accusations, Jill was fed up with the lies, Bill shouted, ***"If this does not stop I am out of here."***

One day Jill and the baby had gone to the grocery store and she over heard these ladies talking, their conversation was so much her life story. Before she knew it she began to say out loud, *"how well do I know this story*." The lady heard her and began to talk with her. The lady told Jill her name was Sue and then she began to witness to her. ***"Do you know the Lord Jesus as your personal savior?"*** she asked. ***"No, my grandmother use to take me to church with her when I was small"*** Jill replied. They began to talk and finally Sue invited Jill to come to church with her. Jill promised she would go to church with her that Friday night.

When Friday night came Bill decided at the last minute to go to a game with some of the guys he worked with. Jill was frantic, ***"you're not going to a game, I know what you are planning on doing." "Jill the guys and I decided at the last minute to go to this game,"*** he replied. ***"Then you won't mind the baby and I coming along,"*** she yelled. ***"You said you were going to church,"*** was his reply. ***"Not tonight, you won't be with her."*** Jill shouted.

Jill decided, ***"I will catch him tonight, if he won't let me go with him I will go on my own."*** Bill got dressed and went to the game with the guys as planned. While dressing for the game the enemy began to talk to Bill,

Silence Is a Root for Shame & Guilt to Grow

"you might as well go on and cheat on your wife, she accuses you anyway, besides, she does not believe anything you tell her."
Jill got one of her friends to watch the baby while she made a trip to the game. On the way to the game she began to listen to the enemy, "***You know he won't be there, I can't wait to hear where he says he's really been, you are going to get the truth tonight.***" When she arrived, she just knew that he would not be there. "***I will just go in look around and wait for him to come home tonight,***" she thought to herself. To Jill amazement Bill was sitting in the second row with the guys he worked with, screaming and laughing. Then as she left the game, Satan began to talk to her again. "***Don't you feel stupid? You missed church tonight just to go to a stupid game and spy on your husband; he probably knew you would come looking for him tonight that is why he is at the game.***"

Satan loves to condemn us.

You know this may sound ridiculous but that is exactly how Satan works. You could have worked on your job six days Monday through Saturday, then on Sunday here comes the enemy, "***you know you are*** *tired, you need to stay home today from church and rest.*" You begin to agree, "*I am sleepy, I have worked all week and tomorrow I have to go right back to work, I need some rest, they probably won't even notice I'm not at church anyway.*" You roll over go back to sleep, then you wake up the service is almost over, the enemy says, "*you know you should have gone to church, now you have to go through all next week without any word.*" Satan loves to condemn us.

Jill called Sue after she got home from the game and apologized for not going to church with her. Sue told her that she would pick her up Sunday morning, she agreed and hung up. That night Jill began to do something she had never done before, she began to talk to God, she said, "*I am so sorry for the way I have been acting towards my husband but I need You to help me. Lord I don't know what to do, I don't know how to stop these feelings, please let me know that You are there, I've heard many things about You. I was told once from my grandmother that You love us with an unconditional love and You will never leave us nor forsake us, I don't know about that because all my life I have been hurt by men, those I love leave me. I am so tired of the way I have been living. Jesus! I need Your help, Amen!*"

Sunday morning Jill got up bright and early, she asked her husband if he would come with her and the baby to church. "*Not today*," her husband replied. "*You go and find Jesus because you really need Him.*" Jill could feel the blood boiling in her and she started to reply but she remembered what she had asked God on Friday night, "***You're right I do need Jesus***," she replied, as she began to get the baby dressed.   Sue came to pick Jill and the baby up for church right on time. Jill introduced Sue to her husband, as they were leaving, "***I would love to take this opportunity to invite you to come with us,***" said Sue.   "***I have other plans today***," Bill replied.

At church Jill really enjoyed the sermon she cried through most of the message. The pastor's message was "***Release & Live.***" He preached that we have to release the burdens and cares that we have been carrying for years, (1 Peter 5:7-8) **"Casting all your care upon him; for he careth for you. Be sober, be vigilant; because your adversary the devil, as a roaring lion, walketh about seeking whom he may devour:** The pastor began to explain how Jesus does not want us to carry our burdens, He wants us to cast them on Him, for He cares for us. Satan wants us to hold onto our burdens because he knows we are not able to carry them.   When you have been holding on to the cares of this world you become weighted down.   Vigilant means to watch, guard, you cannot do that weighted down so you become an easy prey for the devil.   Notice he walks about as a roaring lion, he is not a roaring lion, he deceives and devours many because he is not what he appears.   When the pastor made the altar call she came and gave her heart to God. Jill remembers feeling so good inside, so free, as she put it, "***I am going to tell Bill everything tonight.***"

After putting the baby to bed, Jill asked Bill if they

Soul Ties That Bind

Could talk. *"It's been long overdue,"* Bill replied. **"I gave my heart to God today,"** she stated, *I feel so good and free inside. I know I have not been very easy to live with these last eighteen months, but after hearing the message today and giving my heart to God, I know that I have been changed. I found out today that all the things I have been holding onto all these years I need to release them and let them go. I found out that Satan desires for me to keep silent about my past because he wants to keep me in bondage, but Jesus wants me to release and live. I thought about this and I decided that I would not listen to anymore of the devil lies, if you stop loving me for what happened in my past, you never loved me anyway.*

When I was 10 my parents divorced, I never forgave my father for leaving me, when I turned 14 I was raped. After meeting you and falling in love with you I did not want you to know about my past because I thought you would leave me also. After we were married still listening to Satan lies, I became so jealous, I remembered how we had sex before we were married and I thought, he had sex with me before he married me what's to stop him from being with another woman. I want you to know that after I asked God to forgive me of all my sins today I felt like a new person, now I ask you to forgive me." Bill could hardly speak through the tears, *"I forgive you Jill, I'm sorry for the way I have been acting also, I just never knew you had to go through so much pain. If only you had told me, what*

23

Silence Is a Root for Shame & Guilt to Grow

Do you mean stop loving you? I love you now more than ever. I want to rededicate my life to God, you see I use to be saved and I turned back from following Him, but the change that I see in your life I want it. "

Bill began to pray, "*Lord! I rededicate my life back to You, please come into my heart, I'm coming back home for I have been gone too long, forgive me for all my sins Lord as I surrender my life back to You In Jesus Name.*" With tears of joy streaming down both Bill and Jill face, they begin to ask God to forgive them for the way they had been treating one another and teach them how to really love one another the way He wants them to.

Satan has now lost that strong hold he was holding over Jill's head, why because she exposed the truth. Now he (Satan) must come up with another plan against this marriage because when she told her husband about her past she took back all the power Satan was holding over her. Remember what we said earlier that once you expose it, it loses its strength.

Looking for Love in all the Wrong Places

(John 3:16) For God so loved the world that He gave His only begotten Son that whosoever believeth in Him should not perish but have everlasting life.

Chapter 3

Looking For Love in all The Wrong Places

I always wanted my fathers love and attention (I probably had his love, the only way he knew how to love) and even though he was in the house he was not in my life. He worked, slept and ate there but I never seemed to be able to reach his love and attention I so desired. He never had time for me, he was gone a lot, and he drank a lot. When I grew up I met a man in my 11th grade of high school, we started talking, and he had just gotten out of the US Army. He got a good job; bought a brand new car and I realized this man drank also. It never occurred that I was still looking for the attention and love I never received from my father; I was familiar with the drinking. After we were married he would drink and cheat on me with women. He was gone a lot and he drank a lot, same pattern, and same results.

Gods' plan for man was that he and his mate be saved, have a family, train up their children in the Lord, so they would in turn, train up their children in the Lord and it goes from one generation to the next. Satan always counterfeits or duplicates God so his purpose is for man to never know God. He does not even want you to be married, (he would rather your child be trained to shack up and not make a commitment), but if you are, (his goal then is divorce) he does not want you or your mate to ever know God. They train their children not to know God and it goes from one generation to the next. (Proverbs 22:6) ***"Train up a child in the way he should go: and when he is old, he will not depart from it."*** You see that scripture can be positive or negative. Satan knows that if you train a child to grow up not knowing God, he will not depart from it as well. Train that child up to lie, cheat, steal, beat women, be beaten by men, drink, do drugs, be in gangs, be a homosexual, lesbian, rapist and the list goes on and on, this is Satan plan for your child. This is why so many children are being raised in homes where there is no father; they are being raised most of the time by single moms. Satan targets the children, because whatever you teach them leaves a lifetime impression.

I believe in the black families, this soul tie goes back to when black people were in slavery. Black men would have babies and then they would be separated either the father or the child was sold, not having the responsibility of caring for that child. Today, a lot of black men are made to take care of their children. It comes natural for them to make babies and run off leaving the mother to look to social services or child support agencies to take care of their children. No race is exempt from this behavior but this has been a soul tie that binds a majority of the black males. Satan wants to keep you in bondage, natural freedom came for the black

Looking For Love in all The Wrong Places

man but Satan's strategy is to keep you in bondage, a slave spiritually and naturally. Satan knows that if he can keep your mind there he can keep you there because as Joyce Myers always says "where ever the mind goes the man (body) will follow. Ever wonder why 80% of the men that are incarcerated today are black? Jesus came and died to make all men free but He leaves that choice up to you to accept that freedom. Gods' plan is that when you get married, be equally yoked with a born again believer so your children grows up in a balanced home. *"What is a balanced home*?" you may ask. A balanced home is when the father and mother are in the home and the child is getting the love and discipline from both parents through the word of God. When there is only one parent in the home (and most of the time it is the mother) that child does not get the discipline he/she needs from the mother (some, not all). Satan then takes that and he causes a male child to sometimes seek a mother figure for a companion and not a mate. The male is seeking someone to take care of him and the female is seeking someone she can take care of.

I have seen too many young women looking for love in all the wrong places. Most men that come into their life the woman start out taking care of them (not all but a majority). The woman (9 times out of 10) is the one that has the apartment and the man moves in with her. I talked with a young lady that lived in the projects and she begin to tell me how men would treat them (she had friends that was treated the same way). She told me men would pick them up and if they took them out to eat they expected to go home with them and stay over night, God forbid if they bought them a pair of shoes. She said they looked at them as being less than a lady. "*I've never had a father to show me love,*" she said*, but I know that there is more to love than what he is giving me. I don't like the way he treats me but a piece of a man is better than no man at all.*" This is another lie from Satan. A piece of something is not good for anything unless it is a piece of pie or cake and too many pieces of that can be harmful. God is about wholeness. (John 5:9) *"And immediately the man was made whole, and took up his bed, and walked."*

Women need to hear something, men need to see something and Satan knows this. "*Tell me you love me,*" the woman says, "*show me you love me,*" the man says. A man can be having sex with someone he just met and right in the middle of the act, she will ask him, "**Do you love me?**" I remember when I was married to my first husband and he would treat me like I was nothing, but when we would come together I needed to hear those words. **"I love you."**

Men say, "*You know I love you, you are the only one for me, all those other women don't mean anything to me.*" They tell this same line to Sally, Sue, Donna and Debra because they know this is what you want to hear. He is playing on your feelings and emotions at your expense. Wake up women don't let a man use you like that you were made for greatness, a female, which means there is a fee, males can you pay the price it takes to take care of me? If not, see ya, as they say, and wait on God to bless you. We as women sometimes make bad choices and mistakes when it comes to men, God never makes mistakes.

Ever wonder why women can give a compliment to another woman? That is because she knows it's in us to hear words, and words can build you up or tear you down. Satan knows women love to hear, so if they love to hear, they love to talk. The enemy takes this behavior and just because we are always longing for something to hear we sometimes talk about one another, "***Girl! Did you see what she had on? I would not have worn that to a dog fight. She thinks she's got it going on, well she needs to take a long hard look in the mirror.***" There is a rhyme that says, "***sticks and stones may break my bones but words will never hurt me.***" This is so far from the truth; words can scar a person for a lifetime.
A woman can make a man feel like he is a king or she can make him feel like he is a fool. Words moves us, we see in (1 Samuel 25) how Abigail talked with David after he became angry with her husband Nabal, after sending his young men to ask Nabal to send them food and water. Nabal answered foolishly, (**10**)"***Who is David? And who is the son of Jesse? There be many servants now a days that break away every man from his master. (12) "Shall I take my bread, my water and my flesh that I have killed for my shearers and give it unto men whom I know not whence they be?***" It was told to Abigail (the bible says she was a woman of understanding) she made haste and took food and water to David and began to

minister unto him to stop him from getting revenge on Nabal because he was foolish and refused to help them. She begins to remind David of where God had called him to go and what he called him to be, which was a king. There is a wise man and a foolish man in every man but a woman of understanding can bring out the wisdom in a man, or a foolish woman can bring out the foolishness in a man. The enemy has taken just words and caused many people to commit suicide or murder.

Most men that have been raised in the home with only the mother (some, not all) don't know how to love a woman the way she is supposed to be loved. They know nothing about commitment, responsibility, supporting and protecting a woman, they were never taught and you cannot give something you don't have. They look for the same qualities in that woman that was in their mother, mom bought their sneakers, clothes, and car, paid the insurance and took care of them, and most of the time this is what they expect from you.

I was looking at Joyce Myers one day and she had Dr. Meier, MD on her show, he is a well-known Christian Counselor.   He began to give these statistics:
"1 out of 4 women have been sexually abused."
"1 out of 20 women have been sexually abused by their father."
"1 out of 50 men have been sexually abused by their mother."
Can you see how the enemy can take this and destroy a

Looking For Love in all The Wrong Places

nation of people? Think about it, 1 out of 4 women sexually abused, if they never get free, if they never learn how to forgive, (we will talk about forgiveness later) most of these women will go through life being abused over and over by men. Remember what we said about the familiar place. If she is familiar with this behavior, she will continue to run from one abuser to the next. 1 out of 20 women sexually abused by their father, 1 out of 50 men abused by their mother. He said nothing about the father's or other men abusing their sons also, but I know that this goes on. Now just think about how this behavior continues on with their children and their children's children, and this continues from one generation to the next unless this cycle is broken. Trust me this is exactly what Satan is counting on.

A good father teaches his daughter value, he buys her, her first pair of shoes, he takes her and buys her dresses, he takes care of her, he's there for her when she needs him or someone to talk to, he teaches her how she is to be treated. If she meets a man and he treats her any different than she has been taught she can always come home to daddy. A good father teaches and shows (remember he has to see something) his son to be responsible, to be the protector and provider because he is being that example in the home, he is not just talking it but he is doing it. He disciplines him when he is wrong. Shows him love, teaches him that if you fall and scratch your knee it's all right to cry.

I've seen so many men play that tough role, they are hurting inside or outside but you won't see them cry because daddy says to his son when he gets hurt, "***Suck it up, stop that crying you are tough, take it like a man.***" So throughout life, "***men hide or won't express how they really feel, they won't let you see them cry because they never want you to think that they weak or a sissy.***" Again I say, not all, but a majority.

You may not have had a father in the home to teach you those values. You may even live in a project home, but I want you to know that you have a heavenly Father that loves you more than you could ever imagine and He is there with His arms open wide waiting for you to run to Him. He will teach you those values; He will protect and provide for you. He wants you to know that you were wonderfully and beautifully made. He wants you to be that mature and entire woman/man wanting nothing.

Just wait upon Him; let God bless you with a mate. ***"Girl! I'm looking for a husband."*** Stop looking for a husband, God never intended for you to go looking for a husband, but for you to be found, when we don't wait on God we end up missing our promise. Remember if you wait on Him, you will never lose any time. (Proverbs 18:22) Whoso findeth a wife findeth a good thing, and obtaineth favor of the Lord. Too many times we as women settle for Ishmael and we miss our Isaac. We know in the word of God that Ishmael was not the promised child but Isaac was. God promised Abraham and Sarah that they would have a child. Sarah would not wait for the promise child, (she was going to help God out) God don't need our help, He wants our patience, so she sent her husband Abraham unto her maiden and Ishmael was born (bond child). When Abraham was 100 years old, Isaac the promised child was born. Wait on God; don't miss your promise.

I have mentioned this spirit of homosexuality in the previous chapter this is one of the strongest, rapid growing spirits that must be addressed, and cast out in Jesus name.

Remember if you wait on Him, you will never lose any time.

Pastors allow them to direct the choir, play instruments in church, and even get up before their congregation to bring messages. Satan's goods are in peace as long as we allow this to go on. How can they ever get delivered if we are encouraging what they do? We are putting the armor that Jesus stripped Satan of right back on him. This is how he (Satan) receives his power; we give it to him.

Men always hurt Sandy; her father, growing up her boyfriends, her first and second husband. "*You just can't trust men,* she cried, I *give them my heart they break it every time. I use to think it was me, I thought why can't they love me, what is wrong with me?*" Years later, after she broke up with her second husband, I got a chance to talk with her. "*How have you been,*" I asked. "*I've never been better,* she replied. *I finally figured out why I was having so many problems with men; it's because I am a man trapped in a woman body. Women are just so easy to talk to, they are warm and compassionate, I am just so sorry it took me this long to figure it out. I guess I knew it every since I was in ninth grade, my grandmother always told me I had those masculine tendencies. Maybe I wanted to prove her wrong because she was a lesbian, but you know what they say, the apple doesn't fall too far from the tree."*

Satan always seem to place men, women, situations or obstacles in the lives of those that seemed to have those soul ties of fighting that homosexual spirit, to treat them in a way they run to the same sex for love. Satan says to you, **"Y*ou are a man/woman trapped in a man/woman body*,"** then you open yourself up to that spirit and it enters in. Satan is just seeking for someone that he can devour, that spirit of homosexuality has no limits, color, gender or nationality, many people are tricked into thinking that they were born that way, which is a lie. You were born male or female, you could not choose your gender but you can choose your lifestyle and homosexuality is a lifestyle you do not have to choose. Many women choose that lifestyle (most, not all) because they were raped at a young age. Some were hurt so severely by their father's, others were continually rejected, parents molested some and the list goes on. Satan favorite lines are: "*I knew I was different when I was a child, I am a woman/man trapped in a woman/man body, and I was born this way.*"

Satan does not care about you, all he wants to do is to

Looking For Love in all The Wrong Places

kill, steal and destroy. Jesus came to expose and to destroy the works of Satan. You can be set free from that lifestyle today, the blood of Jesus has made you free, and just do these simple **ABC's:**

A = **Accept Him today as your Lord and Savior.**
B = **Believe that He died for you and rose again.**
C = **Confess your sins and turn away from all Unrighteousness.**

God loves us more than you could ever imagine John 3:16 says He loved us so much that He sent His only begotten Son to die for us (the world). Do you know of anyone that will allow his or her son to die, not just for the world, but a friend or even a family member?

Stronger than the Strong Man

(Luke 11:21-22) "When a strong man, fully armed, guards his own palace, his goods are in peace (satan). (22) But when a stronger than he comes upon him and overcomes him, He(Jesus) takes from him all his armor in which he trusted, and divides his spoils.

Chapter 4

Stronger than the Strong Man

In (Luke 11:21-22) it states that, ***"When a strong man armed keepeth his palace, his goods are in peace: But when a stronger than he shall come upon him, and overcome him, he taketh from him all his armor wherein he trusted, and divideth his spoils."*** Here it talks about two strong men, Satan is the strong man (for he has strong holds in people lives) but Jesus is the stronger man. The stronger man does three things: (1) overcomes the strong man, (2) takes away the armor of the strong man, (3) divides the spoil of the strong man. Jesus has overcome Satan, stripped him of his armor (he has no power, only what you give him) and He divides the spoils. (Luke 10:19-20) ***"Behold, I give unto you <u>power</u> to tread on serpents and scorpions and over all the power of the enemy: and nothing shall by any means hurt you."***

Remember when we talked about Satan walking about as a roaring lion, he has no teeth, Jesus has stripped him of all power and the only power he has is what you give him, you give him nothing he has nothing. He will suggest something to you or plant the idea in your mind (remember we said in chapter one the mind is Satan battleground). (James 4:7) lets us know that if we resist the devil, he will flee from you, but if you listen to him long enough you will end up giving him power, he will talk you right out of your armor. Satan knows that his goods are in peace as long as the people of God are in turmoil, as long as he is able to hold dominion over the hearts of men. He knows his kingdom is sure as long as the people of God mix religion with entertainment and gimmicks and stay involved with the way of the world. Jesus called us to come out from among them and be ye separate. I told you that Satan loves to counterfeit. There is a kingdom of God and there is a kingdom of darkness. Satan rules in the kingdom of darkness, which kingdom do you want to abide in?

Right where you are, if you do not know the Lord, I ask or I beseech you, take this moment and ask God to forgive you of all your sins, ask Him to come into your heart and save you.

If you prayed this prayer God has forgiven you and you have just left the kingdom of darkness and entered into the kingdom of God. You may be all alone right now but I tell you the angels in heaven are rejoicing over you.

Find a spirit filled church and start attending so you can grow into that man or woman of God. Another thing that has happened is that you have broken the chains that the strong man had binding you, that is why when we give our heart to God we feel so free, if we could only see what has just taken place in the spirit.

Stronger than the Strong Man

Sally (I will call her) said, "*I use to wonder why my husband would treat me so bad when he would drink, he was totally opposite when he was sober. You could barely get a word out of him when he wasn't drinking. Oh but when he drank, he would cheat on me with other women, he would fight me, and call me all sorts of names*. One night he began to say to me, "**All you women are just alike.**" "*What do you mean we are all alike? Your mother is a woman too,*" I said. "*I know she is a woman too, and none of you are any good*" he replied. Then he began to tell me how he had come home from school one day and caught his mom in bed with another man. *"I was only six and I will never forget it,"* he said. *"I went and told my dad and he ran my mom away from home, she was gone for awhile before he let her come back home."*

Sally's husband had held this scene in his mind all those years until it had become a strong hold. He was helpless then, there was nothing he could do, but now that he is grown, he will make every woman pay for the way his mom hurt him. There was no trust and every woman to him was just like his mom in his mind, no good. Satan uses these types of situations from the past to control your present and future, he will always bring that ordeal back to your remembrance. You may finish school, get married and go on with your life but if you don't give your heart to God and allow Him to break that strong hold in your life, you will never enjoy or have an abundant life.

Most husbands (not all) that cheat on their wives, when they come home they love to start an argument or even a physical fight because it eases their guilt.

Satan hates women. (Genesis 3:15) *"And I will put enmity (hatred) between thee and the woman, and between thy seed and her seed; it shall bruise thy head, and thou shalt bruise his heel."* It's not that he hates women more than men, he just hates women more in quantity, the quality is the same, it's just more women than there are men, especially in church. There are at least six women to every one man in church.

Women, Satan does not want you to know who you are. You are the one that can bring forth; you are the only one that can birth life. Satan did not even come around until Eve was created for Adam, why? Because the male seed was not any good without the womb of the woman. Jesus began to let us know who we are, remember the woman that was caught in adultery? (John 8:3) They wanted to stone her, they bought her unto Jesus and reminded him of the Mosaic Law, that if a woman is caught in the act of adultery she is to be stoned, (**5**)"*But what sayest thou***?"** the Pharisees asked. Jesus began to stoop down and write on the ground, as if he did not hear them. They continued asking Him, he lifted Himself up and said, (**7**)"**H***e that is without sin among you, let him first cast a stone at her***."** And he stooped down again and wrote on the ground. After hearing and being convicted by their own conscience went out one by one. And Jesus was left alone and the woman standing in the midst. I have found myself being left alone with no one but Jesus, everyone had judged and convicted me and just like he said to that woman, (**10**)"**Woman**, *where are those thine accusers?" hath no man condemned thee?"* (**11**) She answered, "*No man, Lord.*" Jesus said, " N*either do I condemn thee: go and sin no more."*

Let me tell you about the woman with the issue of blood (Mark 5:25). Jesus was on his way to Jairus house because his twelve-year-old daughter was lying at the point of death. There was a woman that had an issue (many of us today have different issues) of blood for twelve years, after making her way through the crowd of people she touched Jesus' garment and was healed immediately, Jesus turned about in the press, and said, (**30**)"*who touched my clothes?"* You can have the faith to stop Jesus also; Jesus wants us to know who we are.

I could go on and on, the woman of Samaria, how there was a need for Jesus to go by her way (Do you have a need today?) (John 4:4). Raising Mary and Martha's brother Lazarus from the dead (John 11:1) Elisabeth was given a son in her old age (Luke 1:7). What I am telling you is that Jesus knows who you are and He has made the way for you to know who you are. Stop saying I can never do this, or I'm not worthy, Jesus made you worthy.

I had a women conference and the Lord had already revealed unto me that this conference would be one where women would open up and release strong holds that was holding them. The Lord truly moved on that Friday night, women were blessed beyond measure; they begin to cry out to God. The service was awesome but I could sense there was more God wanted to do. On that Saturday morning service started at 9:00am, we had three speakers and when I got up to introduce the first speaker I witnessed such a heaviness. I tried to bring the speaker on but this heaviness was so strong I begin to cry out, "**There is someone in here that has such a heavy burden, you need to release it now**." By this time someone in the back begin to say, "*the Lord says to release it, your deliverance is here, and release it*." Immediately, this lady falls out of her seat crying and just lies out on the floor. She cries through the whole service.

After the speakers were finished and the people began to leave (they were calling for snow and ice) there were about eleven of us left there. The Lord told me to have this lady to testify. She got up and this is her testimony: *I was raped as a child from the hands of my brother, uncle and cousins. My mother was very strange, she hated my father and when she would get mad with him she would beat us. I just wanted to grow up and get out of that house.*

I grew up and got into the hands of the wrong man, he would beat me. He would rake the yard before going to work and check for footprints when he would come home. The only place I would go would be to the store with his sister or the grocery store. He would take me upstairs lay me down on the bed and check me, I don't know what he was looking for but if he found it he would beat me.

43

Stronger than the Strong Man

He killed my child! Oh Lord he killed my child! I was pregnant and he beat me because I found out he was staying with another woman. He beat me so bad he caused me to lose my child. He was found guilty for murder. I had to run and abandon my children. I was put in a shelter for 6 months to hide from him. My mother was dying I didn't think I could make it, I did not feel strong enough to take my mothers death. After that I gave my heart to God, started going to church.

I was faithful in church paying my tithes and offering but that was not good enough. The pastor would ask for more and more money, I began working two jobs but that was just not enough. I would come to church so tired from working and the pastor would say that I needed to pay more. I wanted to pay the money in church so bad until I started gambling trying to win just to be able to pay the money to the church. One day I was confronted by my son, he was telling me what I was doing was wrong, finally one day I had gone to get some tickets and I ran into someone that began to tell me that what I was doing was not what God wanted. She took the tickets out of my hands, took me in the corner and prayed for me, she told me to leave and don't look back. I left and did not look back. I found the strength to leave that church. I soon found a church that accepted me for who I was not for what I could do. Since I've joined this church I have been serving God and growing stronger every since.

Speak   From   Your   Position

*(Ephesians 2:6) and raised us up together,
and   made us sit together in heavenly places
in Christ Jesus.*

Not Your Condition

Chapter **5**

Speak from your Position, Not your Condition

(Ephesians 2:6) states that, "*And hath raised us up together, and made us sit together in heavenly places in Christ Jesus:*" Jesus Christ is in the Supreme seat of authority and we have joint seating. We as Christians too many times speak from our condition rather than our position. I have been so guilty of that myself, the enemy shows us a situation or circumstance that looks and I did say looks impossible, right away we begin to speak from the condition we are in and not from the position we sit in. Satan has a plan, he knows the Word of God and he takes pride in using it against us every chance he gets.

Example: You have been feeling very sick; you make an appointment with the doctor. The doctor examines you and he tells you, *"I have some bad news Ms. Right, we have found through the tests we've taken that you have cancer and it has spread throughout your body, we estimate that you only have 6 months to a year to live. We will do everything we possibly can to make this as painless as we can. We also advise you to think about chemotherapy, I am so sorry, if there is anything we can do to help you or if you would like for us to speak with your immediate family please don't hesitate to ask"*.

Soul Ties That Bind

Now you have just been hit with a crisis, *"what are you going to do?"* *Are you going to agree with the doctor? Are you going to hang your head and start making funeral arrangements? Will you call all of your friends and cry on their shoulders while you get angry and charge God foolishly, why did God let this happen to me? What kind of God would let this happen to me?"* This is speaking from your condition. (Mark 11:23-24) *"For verily I say unto you, that whosoever shall say unto this mountain, Be thou removed, and be thou cast into the sea; and shall not doubt in his heart, but shall believe that those things which he saith shall come to pass; he shall have whatsoever he saith."*

First of all the enemy wants you to agree with the doctor, because (Matthew 18:19) says, *"Again I say unto you, that if two of you shall agree on earth as touching anything that they shall ask, it shall be done for them of my father which is in heaven."* Satan wants you to agree with the words from the doctor because he knows that it only takes two of you to agree on earth and it shall be done for you, which can be negative or positive. Next thing he wants you to do is to accept it, when you accept it you will speak it and he knows that you will have whatsoever you say. The Word of God tells us to be swift to hear and slow to speak because we will be snared by our own mouth. (Proverbs 6:2) *"Thou art snared with the words of thy mouth; thou art taken with the words of thy mouth."*

47

Speak from your Position, Not your Condition

Now you have to do something right away, it will seem foolish to the world, trust me I know. After the initial shock, after you have heard what the doctor has to say (because he is speaking from his position) take a deep breath, tell the doctor I appreciate your opinion, but I do not agree nor accept your opinion.

Now you must begin to speak from your POSITION. I am healed by Jesus stripes, (Isaiah 53:5) says, *"But He was wounded for our transgressions, He was bruised for our iniquities: the chastisement of our peace was upon Him: and with His stripes we are healed."* Then you begin to tell yourself I am the healed of God, I walk in divine healing, I shall live and not die, I will only believe the report of the Lord for Isaiah 53:1 says, *"Who hath believed our report? And to whom is the arm of the Lord revealed."* I will not allow this **DECISION** cause me to speak from this **CONDITION** I will only speak from my **POSITION** and that is I sit in heavenly places in Christ Jesus. Get every scripture on healing, get tapes, messages, songs on healing, read them, listen to them, and meditate on them.

I use to work in the medical field, there was a lady that came into the office one day her husband bought her in, she was so very sick, he had to bring her in, in a wheelchair. A friend of mine was her nurse, (Dottie is her name, she is a Christian also), came to me because she knew I was a minister. She said to me with tears in her eyes, *"Please pray for this lady, she is so sick."*

48

after she and her husband came out of the doctor's office, Dottie and I began to pray for her, she had just received bad report from the doctor. I asked her husband if he was born again, he replied that he was, I told him to get every healing scripture that he could find in the bible, write them down and read them to her three times a day until she is strong enough to read them herself. He agreed that he would do that as soon as they got home. We need to learn to take the word just as if it were medicine, there are scriptures that need to get into our spirit (inside) and you will be amazed at the results that shows on the outside.

I was working one day (about six weeks later) and I happened to look up and here comes this lady walking into the office with her husband. "What on earth happened to you?" I said. She said, *"I just want you to know that when we got home I was so sick, I thought I was going to die, my husband went through the Bible and got every healing scripture he could find, and that night he began reading those scriptures to me. He would do this three times a day every day until I got strong enough to read them myself. I began reading them and I began to gain strength, I began to feel better and just look at me now."* Dottie and I began to praise God right there for her healing. So you see you can speak from your position and change your condition. (James 4:7) *"Resist the devil, and he will flee from you."* Satan comes and if we do not resist him, he will begin to speak to us. If we allow him to speak to us his main purpose is to cause you to doubt the word of God. Let me

Speak from your Position, Not your Condition

Let me give you an **Example**:
(Genesis 2:16-17) *"And the Lord God commanded the man, saying, of every tree of the garden thou mayest freely eat: (17) But of the tree of the knowledge of good and evil, thou shalt not eat of it: for in the day that thou eatest thereof thou shalt surely die"*. When God speaks to us He means exactly what He says, and says exactly what He means.

The enemy comes along and he will speak to us so that we will begin to doubt God's word. Look at how he began to speak to Eve, (Genesis 3:1) *"And he (Satan) said unto the woman, Yea, hath God said, Ye shall not eat of every tree of the garden?" (5) For God doth know that in the day ye eat thereof, then your eyes shall be opened, and ye shall be as gods, knowing good and evil. (6) And when the woman saw that the tree was good for food, and that is was pleasant to the eyes, and a tree to be desired to make one wise, she took of the fruit thereof, and did eat, and gave also unto her husband with her; and he did eat."* First of all they (Adam and Eve) had no business even at the tree. If you know you are forbidden to have something why do you go to the very thing that is forbidden? Every time we do this we are going on Satan territory, you can count on him to be where you are forbidden to be.

He starts out by questioning what God said to her. Then he began to plant the seed in her mind that God was keeping something from her, and she had to have had those thoughts to even be at the forbidden tree.

Soul Ties That Bind

The Bible tells us in (I John 2:16) *"For all that is in the world, the lust of the flesh, and the lust of the eyes, and the pride of life, is not of the Father (GOD), but is of the world (Satan)."* Satan will use one of these weapons on you, I call them the three hit men and if you are not focused one of them will assassinate (to murder, to destroy or injure treacherously) you. I have seen many men brought down (Christians, Pastors, Leaders, Unbelievers as well) by these hit men. I have seen pastors leave their ministry and wives for the other WOMAN; I've even seen them commit spiritual incest with their sons and daughters in the gospel. Leaders stop loving and teaching the word of God for MONEY. Christians stop following God because of PRIDE. Because Eve chose to believe the lying thoughts that Satan put in her mind rather than God's word, she was deceived and hit by all three. (Gen. 3:6)

1). And when the woman saw that the tree was good for food (**LUST OF THE FLESH**).

2). And that it was pleasant to the eyes (**LUST OF THE EYE**).

3). And a tree to be desired to make one wise (**PRIDE OF LIFE).** Please don't underestimate the power of the devil to deceive. Don't get me wrong I give no glory to the devil, for that is exactly what he wants, glory and praise, I am just exposing him for who he is. Jesus said, " *And have no fellowship with the unfruitful works of darkness, but rather expose them* (Ehp. 5:11)."

The bible lets us know that we go from faith to faith; I want you to see this as from grade to grade. When you

Speak from your Position, Not your Condition

were in school you were taught and then ever so often you were tested to see how much you have learned. This testing allows the teacher to see how much you have remembered or advanced while being taught. When she test you and you pass the test, (some passes with flying colors, some passes, others barely passes and then there are those that fail the test), then you are promoted to the next grade, if you keep failing then you are held back. Well, we are sometimes tested to see how much we have advanced or remember what we have been taught. We go to Sunday school, we hear the minister preach and teach us the word of God, now here comes the test. (Psalms 7:9) lets us know that God tests our heart. He also allows trials to come our way to make us strong. (I Peter 4:12-13) **"Beloved, think it not strange concerning the fiery (painful) trial which is to try you, as though some strange** thing **happened unto you: But rejoice, inasmuch as ye are partakers of Christ's sufferings; that, when his glory shall be revealed, ye may be glad also with exceeding joy."** So you see we should not think it strange when we go through trials and believe me sometimes they are fiery (painful) trials. We should rejoice and be exceedingly glad because then we know that His glory shall be revealed in us.

Speak from your position. Let the devil know that you know who you are and what your rights are. Have you ever seen a police person not walking in their authority? I tell you if an 18 wheeler truck was coming down the street and he saw a policeman with his hand outstretched to stop him, trust me he will squeal those tires trying to stop because no matter how small that officer may be that trucker recognizes authority. That is how it should be with us; we should be able to change the atmosphere when we walk into a room because we have authority over every demonic spirit. Those spirits should be just like that trucker squealing to get out of our way because he recognizes our authority. It is only when we do not know who we are that the enemy does not respond and believe me Satan knows when you don't know who you are.

I must tell you the story of the Shunammite woman in (II Kings **4:8).** If ever there was a woman that spoke from her position and not her condition it was this woman. Elisha the prophet, would often pass through Shunem, there was, the bible calls her a great woman. This woman would compel him to eat, and when he would go through Shunem, he would always stop by her house to eat bread. She said to her husband, **(9)** *"I perceive that this is a holy man of God, which passeth by us continually. (10) "Let us make a little chamber, I pray thee, on the wall; and let us set for him there a bed, and a table, and a stool and a candlestick, and it shall be, when he cometh to us, that he shall turn in thither."*

One day when he came and went into the chambers that was built for him, he said to Gehazi his servant, call this Shunammite. When he called her she came and stood before Elisha. He said unto her, **(13)**"*What can I do for you for all your hospitality.*" She told him she was satisfied. Gehazi told Elisha that she had no child and her husband was old. Elisha called her to him a second time and told her that she would embrace a son in nine months. Her reply was, **(16)** *"Nay, my lord, thou man of God, do not lie unto thine handmaid."*

Now I want to stop right here for a moment to let you know that back then, every woman wanted a child. You were looked upon as being less than a woman if you did not have a child, moreover, every woman wanted to have a male child, knowing that the Messiah was promised to be born through a woman. The next negative thing, her husband was old so when Elisha told her that in nine months she would embrace a son, she did not want to get her hopes up so she asked him not to lie to her.

Well, the woman conceived and had a son in the nine months exactly like Elisha promised. The child grew and one day he went out to his father to the reapers. He said to his father, "my head, my head." His father sent him to his mother; he sat on her knees till noon, and then died.

What do you do when the promise dies? Have you ever believed God for something and you receive it and it seems as if it dies. It may be healing, salvation for a loved one, finances, etc. Just when you thought you were healed, here comes that sickness again. God saved your loved one then they backslide. Things were going pretty good, bills were being paid, not in a financial bind then all of a sudden you and your wife is laid off work. God promised us all these things Healing, Salvation for our household, every need supplied, so now what do you do? It seems as if the promise

Speak from your Position, Not your Condition

has died, or you have not received the promise yet. Do you speak from your position or has the enemy caused you to look at the situation around you and you start speaking from your condition?

When you speak from your position you speak faith, remember what faith is, the substance of things hoped for, the evidence of things not seen. When you speak from your condition you speak doubt and unbelief, you speak on the things that are seen, not hoped for. Take that promise and lay it before God and stretch out on it. You may have to pray more than one time but keep on praying and stretching out on God's promises, life will come, your promise will come to pass.

That Shunammite woman did not start charging God foolishly, she did not start complaining, saying, "*I told him not to lie to me, I knew this would happen. Lord I built this man a chamber to stay in and you let this happen to me.*" She did not start making funeral arrangements. The bible says she went up and laid her son on the man of God bed and shut the door. Instead of her crying to her husband that the child was dead, she called her husband and said, " *Please send me one of the young men and one of the donkeys that I may run to the man of God and come back.*" Always run to God, never run from Him. Her husband said, "W*hy are you going to him today? It is neither the New Moon nor the Sabbath.*" And she said, "*IT IS WELL.*" This is a woman that is speaking from her position and not her condition. When we can pass this test

55

(remember we talked about the fiery trials) we will see miracles, His glory. Then she said to her servant, **(24)"Drive and go forward; do not slow down for me unless I tell you."** We must continue to go forward when we are faced with adversity, isn't it amazing how we always do the opposite, we stop and go backwards, we slow down, we stop praying, reading our word, stop praising God.

So she went to the man of God, when he saw her coming afar off he told his servant to go and meet her and say to her, **(26)"Is it well with you? Is it well with your husband? Is it well with the child?"** She did not answer and say, "no, everything is not all right, my son is dead and I told you in the beginning not to lie to me. Everything was fine just the way it was. I wish I had never met you, and God knows I wish I had never invited you into my house." That is speaking from your condition, but this great woman spoke from her position and said, **"IT IS WELL."**

God had to move in this situation, because faith moves God. Our crying, complaining or murmuring does not move God, our faith does. She began to say to the man of God, **"Did I ask you for a son my lord? Did not I say, do not deceive me?** Elisha told his servant to take his staff and go to this woman house and if you meet anyone do not speak to them and if they speak to you do not take the time to speak to them, but lay my staff on the face of the child. When Elisha got there the child was

Speak from your Position, Not your Condition

Dead lying on his bed.   He went in and shut the door Behind him and prayed to the Lord.   He went up and lay on the child, and put his mouth on his mouth, his eyes on his eyes and his hands on his hands, and he stretched out on that child and the flesh of that child became warm.

He returned walking back and forth in the house, and again went up and stretched himself on him, then the child sneezed seven times, and the child opened his eyes. He then called his servant and said, (**36**)**"Call this Shunammite woman,"** and when she came in to him, he said, **"Pick up your son."**   She went in fell at his feet, bowed to the ground, then she picked up her son (promise) and went out.

I love reading this passage in the bible because it always remind me that when a storm comes our way we can speak peace to that storm.   We have peace in us, Jesus said, (John 14:27) **"Peace, I leave with you, my peace I give unto you: not as the world giveth, give I unto you, let not your heart be troubled, neither let it be afraid."**   We don't have peace like the world; the world's peace is when everything is going well, money in the bank, food, clothes, health and etc.   Let something go wrong, their peace is gone.   If you do not Know peace, you will have No peace.   So you see we have peace in us, therefore, we can speak peace in the midst of any storm, situation or circumstance.   Satan depends on us to look at the boisterous sea, and allow fear to grip our hearts, in turn, hoping we will speak from that condition;

remember Satan knows that you will have whatsoever you say.   That is why the word of God tells us to be Swift to hear, slow to speak. Slow to wrath (James 1:19).

I challenge you from this day forward when trouble, situations, problems, storms or circumstances (really they are the cares of this world) come your way, take a deep breath, pull yourself together knowing that you have the power to call those things that be not as though they were (Romans 4:17).   Then say out loud, *"I will take this opportunity to SPEAK FROM MY POSITION AND NOT MY CONDITION."*

The Danger of Unforgiveness

(Mark 11:25-26) And whenever you stand praying, if you have anything against anyone, forgive him that your father in heaven may also forgive you your trespasses. (26) But if you do not forgive, neither will your Father in heaven forgive your trespasses.

Chapter 6

The Danger of Unforgiveness

After I gave my heart to God, I thought I had forgiven my dad. Remember in chapter three, how I felt like I never had his love or attention. I truly thought those feelings were gone. Oh! How wrong I was. When my father went to the hospital in 1994, he was diagnosed with prostate cancer. The doctor said it had spread throughout his bones and there was nothing else they could do for him.

Early one rainy Saturday morning, my phone rang, it was my father, ***"Come over and bring your bible,"*** he said. I stayed right next door to my parents, so I got my bible thinking he wanted me to pray for him. When I got there he said to me, ***"I want to be saved."*** My parents knew how much I loved God; they would come to most of my speaking engagements, especially if it were close to where we lived. I was so excited I had to get myself together and before I could answer him, he said, ***"What do I need to do?"*** I began to turn to

Soul Ties That Bind

Romans 10:9-13;   I read those scriptures to him, then I said to him, repeat this prayer after me. *"Lord, I come before you a sinner, I'm sorry and I am asking You to forgive me of all my sins, I believe in my heart that God has raised You from the dead.   Lord come into my heart and save me and I will live for You for the rest of my life."*

After my father prayed that prayer, I prayed for him and tears began to roll down his face. I knew my dad was saved, I was so thankful that he had given his heart to the Lord and so grateful to God that my life was pleasing enough for him to ask me to introduce him to salvation.   I was so excited and happy for my dad.

My dad's health declined more and more and because I had some experience in the medical field he wanted me to do everything for him. He would call for me all through the day and night. I would be so tired; I went over there so much until I had a little trail from my house to his house. It was as if he did not trust anyone else to take care of him, not even my mom. I remember one day I had to go out of town and he did not want me to go, **Who will give me my medicine,"** he said**. "Mom can give you your medicine,"** I said. **"She can't do it like you can,"** he replied. **"Well she has to give it to you today because I have to go,"** I said.   Then I started noticing these feelings I was having, I tried to overlook them but they were too obvious. One day I mentioned that I would be going out of town for a few days. **"*You can't go out of town for a few days, I need you here with***

The Danger of Unforgiveness

me, "my father said.   I got so angry I stormed out of the door.   My mother came behind me to find out if I was all right. *"No I'm not all right, I don't know what he means when he says he needs me, where was he when I needed him?   He's never been there for me.*" I shouted.   After my mom left, I begin to pray and the Lord let me know that I was holding Unforgiveness towards my father.   I thought to myself, *"I'm saved, I don't have Unforgiveness in my heart, I got over that years ago."*

I did not even call him dad, his name was Otis and when I was 12, I started calling him O. All my sisters and brothers called him daddy except me. I really did not feel that he loved me as a father so why call him that? He never spent any time with me, other than scratching his head; he loved for me or anyone to scratch his head.

He wanted me to come over and just sit with him; I would go over pray and read the bible to him. I can remember how afraid he was of dying and the more I would pray and read to him the more I would see that fear turn into faith in God. When he could no longer swallow his food and the doctor had to put a feeding tube in, he really thought that I should be there every minute of the day. *"I love you and no one else can take care of me like you can, just stick with me I'm going to take care of you,"* he said. I was shocked, this was the first time I had ever heard him say those words, especially I LOVE YOU. I thought to myself, *"It's a little too late for that now."*   Don't get me wrong I loved my dad and I would do anything for him but I kept having these feelings going on inside of me.

"Where have you been?" my dad asked one Saturday as we were both driving up. *"I had to work this morning,"* I said. My mom, sisters and my dad were just getting back from shopping. *"I was looking for you because I wanted to take you shopping to buy you something,"* he said. He looked so exhausted, "*Just take me another day*," I replied. *"No I want to take you today,"* he insisted. Finally, seeing how persistent he was I said all right. We went to the department store and he insisted on coming in with me, I was just going to go in and grab something so I could get him home because he was so weak. I hurriedly picked up something, *"I like this outfit,"* I said. *"Try it on,"* he said. *"Oh! I know it fits*," I said, trying to rush. *"I want you to try it on"*, he said. I went to try the outfit on and when I came out of the fitting room; my dad was leaning over the dress racks as if he would pass out. *"That looks so good on you,"* he said, with pain in his eyes. I looked at my dad and tears began to fill my eyes, right then and there I started praying, in my heart I truly forgave my dad that day. I began to see life in a different way, I felt light, as if a burden had been lifted off my shoulders.

The Lord let me see how dangerous it was for me to hold Unforgiveness; you can never go forward or be healed until you forgive. I also realized that if I did not

The Danger of Unforgiveness

forgive, God would not forgive me. Satan loves for us to hold Unforgiveness in our hearts. He wants us to say, ***"I don't care what he or she does, no matter how much they ask me to forgive them, I'm never going to forgive them for what they said, did or the way they hurt me."*** Guess what? Your heavenly Father will not forgive you, until you forgive. This is what Satan is counting on you to do. (Matthew 6:14-15) ***"For if you forgive men their trespasses, your heavenly Father will also forgive you: (15) But if ye forgive not men their trespasses, neither will your Father forgive your trespasses."***

I felt so good after I forgave my dad, I was not just saying it with my mouth but I truly forgave him in my heart. ***"Well I can forgive but I can't forget,"*** you may say. Let me tell you what God will do for you when you forgive from your heart, you are right you don't forget, but it doesn't hurt anymore when you remember it. Unforgiveness will cause pain; hurt and depression even when we think about it. Some people go to their graves with Unforgiveness in their hearts. I promise you, if you let it go and forgive, you will witness such a freedom and healing. You may say, **"What if they are deceased, married, left town with no address?"** Write them a letter, read it out loud when you get alone, then tear the letter up and throw it away.

My husband and I did a 3-night crusade in my hometown. There was a young lady in that service on the first night and the Lord led me to minister to her. **"I never got a chance to say goodbye to my husband. I**

64

Soul Ties That Bind

left the hospital to run home just for a minute and when I got back he was gone (died), there was some things I wanted to forgive him of, I miss him so much, I feel like I just can't go on with life," this young lady said. *"Write him a letter, and tell him everything that you were not able to tell him, read the letter out loud as if you were reading it to him, then destroy it,"* I said. The next night she was there, she came up to me after service and she shared with me that immediately after that service she went home and wrote the letter, *"I felt so good after writing and reading that letter last night, can I write another one tonight?"* she asked. *"Sure, as many as it takes,"* I said. That was two years ago, that young lady is now married again.

My father passed away about three months after I truly forgave him. I had no regrets or guilt feelings when he died because I did everything I could for him. Now I must explain to you what took place after forgiving my dad.

My ex-husband had died of a massive heart attack 7 years earlier; he was not good to me or the children at all. Like I said in chapter three he drank a lot, was gone a lot, would fight me and he cheated with other women. God totally set me free from that bondage, but if I had not forgiven my dad I would never have met my second husband.

Listen to this; six (number of man) months after my dad died I met this man. We started talking, I begin to like him a lot, but he was not the one for me. Then seven (number of complete) months later I met my

The Danger of Unforgiveness

husband, a true man of God. I found out that God was not about to let me marry this man with all this unforgiveness I had in my heart. Let me explain something to you, God loves His sons and daughters and He will not put you with them to hurt them. I had to get rid of the Unforgiveness first, and then God blessed me with a man that truly loves Him and me. So you see you may also be holding up blessings because of Unforgiveness.

In her own words here is a testimony of Pastor Felicia Mock a very dear friend of mine that dealt with the danger of Unforgiveness and how it tried to destroy her:

Hello my name is Felicia and I want to share with you my testimony about the danger of Unforgiveness in your heart. About seven years ago being saved and working for the Lord, I had these "episodes" I would call them of self hatred and low self esteem, it would torment my mind so much that I would go to bed and want to sit in the dark. I knew I loved God with all my heart or so I thought.

One day as I lay in my bed dealing with one of these severe "episodes" I decided to hurt myself, the pain I felt was unbearable. I loved my family and friends too much to ever hurt them with total suicide, so I decided I would just hurt myself. I went to the bathroom and got my eyebrow blade and began to write across my belly "I HATE YOU." Yes, it did hurt and blood was dripping and I looked at myself in the mirror and said, "God Help Me!" I heard the Lord say, "Felicia you have Unforgiveness in your heart, you don't hate yourself, you hate all that was done to you and it's in your heart." I began to speak with the Lord that day like I never have before; He talked with me as if He was sitting on the bed holding my hand, explaining Unforgiveness to me.

66

Soul Ties That Bind

I had been holding so much pain for such a long time until it became a part of me.   It was as if I had trapped the man that raped me, the husband that beat and battered me, the family and so called friends in my heart, and they were living there.   So I hated them inside for what they had done to me.   Everyone that had ever hurt me deeply lived on in my heart and some of these people died years ago but were very much alive in my heart. Now I had to let go and release them to God that day. The Lord walked me through a deliverance I have never seen before, forgiveness "pure and genuine" as I called them out name by name, everyone I forgave and God took them out of my
heart like a splinter in a finger leaving no pain or discomfort behind.   From that day forward I WAS ON A NEW PATH TO A HEALTHY WALK IN CHRIST, TOTALLY FREE, loving myself and others the way Christ ordained it to be.

With Choices Comes Consequences

(Joshua 24:15) And if it seem evil unto you to serve the Lord, Choose you this day whom ye will serve; whether the gods which your fathers served that were on the other side of the flood, or the gods of the Amorites, in whose land ye dwell: but as for me and my

Chapter **7**

With Choices Comes Consequences

With every choice that we make there comes consequences with that choice, God gave us our own free will, which means He gave us the right to choose. God will not make us serve Him, that would be like having a puppet and He pulls the string and we do as He says, no, God allows us to make up our own minds as to whether we will serve Him or not. (Joshua 24:15) says, *"And if it seems evil unto you to serve the Lord, choose you this day whom ye will serve"*.

If you were to get pregnant you choose to have that child or have an abortion. Satan comes to you when you get pregnant and whispers in your ear. *"You know you don't have the time or money to have a baby, you know your babies father said he did not want any children, your family will be disappointed in you, they won't love you any more. What you need to do is go on and get rid of this baby right now, besides he will be better off."* This is just some of the things Satan tells you. He wants you to get rid of this child because you may have an Apostle, Prophet, Evangelist, Pastor or Teacher inside of you. I have heard many women say, "I *wonder what my baby would have been like had I kept him/her. I still have nightmares about them.*" One lady said, *"God want forgive me because I am a murderer, I killed my children."*

People that choose to steal, lie, cheat, kill, and I could go on and on, they have to suffer the consequences for all their actions. If the thief, liar, cheat, murderer is caught they pay the consequences. A lot of times people try to blame God for their actions. They steal and get caught, go to jail and say that God doesn't love them, if He did, he would not have permitted them to go to jail. (Galatians 6:7) says, *"Be not deceived; God is not mocked (laughing) whatsoever a man soweth, that shall he also reap."* Satan always shows you how to do what is wrong and allow you to think you can get away with it, but he never shows you the out come. He plants these thoughts in your mind, plan the whole ordeal out, you think you have the perfect plan (Remember I told you your mind is Satan battleground). (John 10:10) says, *"The thief (Satan) cometh not, but for to steal, and to kill, and to destroy.* Satan does not care about you or me. He needs a body to carry out his plans. He will lead you out on a limb and once you get there he will leave you. Just consider the consequences before you decide to do that which is wrong for you shall surely pay for your actions.

Many people that are addicted to drugs are also looking for love in all the wrong places; you have many people that seem to be very intelligent that find themselves hooked on drugs. They say to themselves,

With Choices Comes Consequences

"I'm too smart to get hooked, I can try it and quit when ever I want to." You are the ones Satan looks for, because he knows that, you play the Game, the Game play the Game, then the Game plays you. It is called the "BIG LIE" why? Because the first time you use it, the high that you get, you never get it again, so Satan knows that you will go back time after time trying to get that same high you first experienced. You continue to seek this feeling falling deeper and deeper into his (Satan) trap until you are hooked; now you have no control because your very soul is tied to this drug and you will do anything to get it. I have come in contact with people that would sell their body, children, home, car, clothes or whatever they could find. They steal, lie, cheat and even kill, they are no longer in control, and they become someone that they don't even know. They say to themselves today I will quit, I must do this for my children but the desire and urge won't let them quit. They find themselves doing whatever it takes to get the drugs. This is a STRONGHOLD!

You don't have to make the wrong choices, it starts out as fun, *"Come on and try this it will make you feel good. I want to take you on this trip with me it will make* you *forget all about your troubles,"* your friend says. What they don't tell you is that your troubles are just beginning. Most people that choose to try drugs soon become a slave to it. There are some people that get addicted to drugs through prescribed medicine, addiction is addiction and they all will pull you into bondage.

Soul Ties That Bind

Here is a story in her own words of a beautiful young lady that chose to try drugs; her name is Marion Johnson:

I will call this true life story "A man with "that Girl" for that is how exactly I viewed it, I pray that once you read the choices that I made and the consequences that I endured you will never choose to go down that same path that I took.
I was a 23 years old, young, single, black female with everything I wanted.   At least that's what I thought; my own home, nice car, great career, successful in everything I did, money saved in the bank in case of emergencies, plenty of clothes, shoes, and accessories to match, every kind of credit card offered, I had it, went to church on Sundays.   I even had a wonderful family who loved me dearly.   You couldn't ask for a better life than what I had, except for one thing.   I was in love with a man who wasn't in love with me, and that was devastating to me. Sitting in my home one Super Bowl Sunday (I was not able to get out to enjoy the Super Bowl festivities because of a blizzard).   I had snow blown up to my door about 36 inches, there I was content being in my cozy warm place, not realizing that the blizzard was about to bring a man into my life that would devastate me even more than I was already.   Quite handsome this young man was, and he always had admired me and wanted me for his girlfriend, but I would never give him any time.   When he walked through the door, he stated that he was told that I was by myself and he wanted to know if I wanted some company.   Naturally being lonely, my first response was, "sure come on in make your self at home."   Not knowing that the statement literally came to pass. When that man walked through that threshold he never left. Little to my surprise this man had a package with him, and as we grew closer together through time he began to reveal this package to me, the package was that "Girl", as most people called her.   One night while we sat in my

72

With Choices Come Consequences

Home, yes this man moved in and told me that he would take care of me, and never hurt me like the man whom I really loved did. He told me that he would love me for me, and I didn't have to change. The handsome young man pulled out that "Girl", laid her across the table, smooth she was, white as pure snow, and when you looked at her a certain way she had a sparkle about her. The young man seemed to be so relaxed, loving and affectionate as he took in that "Girl" through his nostril, and then placed her in his mouth. She came in different forms, shapes and sizes, some powdered and some like tiny rocks on the beach. It was truly amazing to me because I had never seen anything like this in my life. It was amazing to me how he moved with her and how she treated him so smooth. Out of curiosity I asked him if I could try some of what he had, quickly with a stern voice, he said to me, "no baby, this isn't something that a beautiful young woman should be engaging in." One day while the young man wasn't home, I found out where he kept "That Girl". I pulled her out, spread her across the table as I'd seen the young man do, place some in my mouth, as well as my nostrils, which became numb. I began to examine the "Girl" that was shaped like tiny rocks on the beach, its color was that of ivory, and yet so smooth looking. It too had a glaze if you looked at in a certain way. That "Girl" came with all the tools needed to engage her with. I began to engage myself with that "Girl" shaped like tiny rocks by using the tools used for smoking, as I had seen the young man do. Oh! The way it made me feel was awesome, better than sex it was, I didn't have a care in the world, better yet I could take on the world. I felt sexy, affectionate, loved and relaxed, while my heart raced so fast, like it was about to beat out of my chest, the longer I held that "Girl" in the higher I would get, and when I felt I couldn't go any higher I released it into the air. My ears began to ring sweet love melodies and "that Girl" was taking me for a smooth ride. She took me higher, and higher, and higher.

73

Soul Ties That Bind

By the time the young man got home I was feeling pretty good. When the young man found out what I had been into, he was not too happy. Now I know why. I had used "that Girl" the young man had been depending on. Little did I know that "that Girl" was going to control me; why because I was running after that first feeling I had when that "Girl" came into my life. I craved her day and night, when I was asleep I dreamed of how I would get more of her. On my job I would think about getting home so that I could get her in my system. I craved the way she made me feel when I was with her, day in and day out. From that day on for 3 years, "that Girl" was apart of my life. She was in control of everything. She made you spend money that you had and that you didn't have; she kept you up all night long until the break of dawn. She was surely a nighttime girl. At first I used her casually, and then I became addicted. I had to have "that Girl" everyday. I had "that Girl" when the young man was home, and when he wasn't, because he always made sure there was just enough of her to help me get through the day while he worked. Eventually the young man asked me to marry him. Not yet over the devastation of the man that I loved that didn't love me. I thought to myself, this is any opportunity to show that man that didn't love me that I could get me a husband and he would love me for me, as well as, take care of me. I wanted to hurt him as bad as he had hurt me. Little did I know, when I said yes to the proposal, not only was I marrying the young man, but I was marrying "that Girl" as well, and she was in control of the two of us.

When I said, "I do" to the young man, "that Girl" said "yes" to both of us. "That Girl" became a part of both of our lives. Every day we took "that Girl" in, we used her and she controlled us. My husband worked every day, and made good money, so it wasn't as hard on us as if we didn't have any money to support our habit. After awhile I quit my job and stayed at home with "that Girl" by my side. Little did I know it gave me

74

With Choices Come Consequences

more room for the devil to take control; eventually we opened our home to the supplier of "that Girl", and his girlfriend. Now we always had company, because people would come to buy "that Girl" as well as have a party with "that Girl". My husband would never let me mingle with the people. As the days passed by, I thought that I was over that man who devastated me; and I thought that I could grow to love the man that I was with, but it didn't work like that. When I did sleep I would think about him, and when I was home alone I thought about him, saying to myself if I was with him I wouldn't be in this shape, because he wasn't that type of person. Now, every day my husband and I would fight over that man, because he would accuse me of seeing him or being with him when I wasn't at home. We began to argue about everything now. He even started accusing me of taking his "Girl" when he wasn't around. Now that we didn't have to pay money for "that Girl" she really controlled my husband until sometimes he was crazy. He would look all over the floor, tearing up furniture, looking behind pictures on the walls, tearing the curtains off the windows, because he thought "that Girl" was there, she never was.

The more of "that Girl" we used the more we wanted. I wouldn't sleep; I wouldn't even eat for days and months at a time. Now, I began to wear the bruises from "that Girl" when she would cause the arguments and they became physical. I remember one night my husband had been out all night with that "Girl", because he wanted her all to himself. When he came home the next morning, I questioned him about being out, next thing I remember he grabbed me by my neck and lifted me up off of the floor, and I remember my spine hitting the hinges of our guest bedroom. I fell to the floor in a lifeless motion, I just knew I was dead. I really didn't know what had happened to me. He just walked away, didn't even try to help me up or anything, I was once again devastated by what was happening. I remember saying to him, I hate you and called him a dirty name.

Soul Ties That Bind

After the fights, we would makeup and get that "Girl" it seemed that it made things better until she was all gone and we needed more of her. Then the fighting would start all over again. One day when my husband came home from a hard day at work, I hadn't cooked anything. Sometimes he would like to eat before he used "that Girl". He said something to me and I responded with a smart answer, then he accused me of being with the man I really loved, he accused me of being too fat, and he didn't want me anymore. The next thing I remember was being in the floor where this man stomped me with his steel toe work boots; once again he had his hands around my neck trying to strangle me as I found myself fighting back to stay alive. This is how I learned how to fight, because I had to fight everyday for almost a year to stay alive. When we did sleep, he would make me sleep close to him, as he held me in his arms, or he would sleep on his stomach and have me to wrap my arms around him. This part of the marriage I loved, because we were not fighting, it made me feel that he really did love me, plus, I wanted to make my marriage work, I loved it because he was affectionate to me. So I got to the place that I wasn't able to sleep if he wasn't in the bed with me. I'm still like that today. How lovely I felt until the fighting started again. I would wear the bruises like garments from my head to my toes. That's what "that Girl" will do, when she controls you. I got to the place where I didn't care about how I looked, or what I would put on, sometimes I would wear the same thing for days. I had to pass a mirror after one of our fights and I saw just how bad I looked. That's what "that Girl" will do, when she controls you.

I heard a young lady crying, and screaming as though someone was murdering her. When my husband opened the door to see what was going on, he saw that it was the supplier of that "Girl" and his girlfriend, they were fighting and he was trying to kill her before my very eyes. How devastating that was because she was lying in a pool of blood, face beaten badly, and needed some medical care. Of course you know when "that Girl" is around there is no medical care unless you give it to

With Choices Comes Consequence

yourself. My husband stepped into the hallway to pull the supplier off the young lady. He told me when he got his hands on the supplier and pulls him off of her; I was to drag her as quickly as I could into the room where I was and lock the door until he returned. I was obedient to his commands. The strange thing to me was when my husband was doing that "Girl" he was so protective of me and didn't want anyone to hurt me. I had no self-esteem by this time; I didn't even love my own self. It was a long night ahead, but I never let it stop me from that "Girl" and that "Girl" never left me alone. After I cleaned up the young lady as best I could, then she and I shared that "Girl". As I began to console the young lady, very strange feeling came over me. I began to feel as though I didn't want to live, and this feeling got stronger and stronger the more of that "Girl" that I would use.

I began to hear voices and they were strong and demanding. One of the voices said to me "go into the bathroom, lock the door, look in the medicine cabinet and get your husbands razor. As I listened to the voice, I proceeded to get a white sheet and line the bathtub; I locked the bathroom door so no one could get in. I sat down in the bathtub, and I began to cut my left wrist first, nothing happened, no blood would come out, so I got up and stepped out of the bathtub, got another brand new razor. I got back in the bathtub, this time lying in a prostrate position, tried to cut my right wrist. I lay there thinking surely I was going to bleed to death and I wouldn't have to endure this pain and devastation that I was going through. To my surprise when I looked no blood had come out of my wrist. This I couldn't understand, so I began to cry and scream with a loud voice, "just take me, I don't want to live like this anymore." I lay there weeping in the bathtub; I covered myself in the white sheet in hopes to smother myself to death. Nothing would work, my husband broke into the bathroom and he was so angry with me. He began to curse me, tell me how stupid I was, and he didn't need a weak woman, he needed someone that was going to

Soul Ties That Bind

be strong in this thing with him. He walked away from me once again while I was in a hurting state, he didn't even bother to hold or comfort me. About that time, the young lady that was in the room with me came into the bathroom to comfort and console me. Of course you know what she had, yes, it was that "Girl" she said these words, "come on girlfriend, you need this "Girl". I remember by this point I had no desire to mess with that "Girl". I tried to let her go but she wouldn't let me go. No matter how much I tried to stay away from that "Girl" her scent, taste and the way she made me feel, would never leave me. That "Girl" was in control, and it got worse.

The supplier and his girlfriend finally moved out of our home, and by this time I was tired of that "Girl", fighting, and the man with that "Girl", I was just tired of everything, the whole scene. I would lie in bed at night and try to figure out how I was going to get out of this situation, because I couldn't just walk away. My husband had told me one time before that if I left him he would find me, no matter where I would go. I remember trying to figure out how I was going to kill him and get away with, because I was just tired, tired, tired, and weary, devastated, jobless, no where to turn to and especially tried of that "Girl" and what she was doing to my life.

One day when I was home alone, something just said to me pack up everything, take what belongs to you and run for your life. Things can't get any worse. So I did, I packed up everything that belonged to me which was practically everything, called my mother and told her that I was leaving and I needed her to help me. She and my father rented a truck and storage for me to put my stuff in. They made room in their home for me to put my bedroom suite. I wanted to leave my husband a note, but I knew that would defeat the purpose of me leaving. So I took my car and left, tears rolled down my face, but I had to leave or I would surely die in this place, either through that "Girl" or the fighting

78

With Choices Come Consequences

would surely take me out.   I was fine until nighttime came and it was time to go to bed.   I missed his arms being wrapped

around me to make me feel loved and secure.   I wasn't able to sleep, so within a matter of hours, I got in my car, drove to where we lived and sat in the car on the corner.   While sitting there I saw something to my surprise, my husband and another women going in our home together.   I knew it was only because of that "Girl" that she was there and I wasn't.   So I couldn't take it any longer, I drove up the driveway, and got out, walked in the house has if I had never left or done anything.   Within 24hrs, I moved just my bedroom suite back in the house.   I left everything else in storage there.   I found myself right back doing the very thing that I was trying to get away from.

I thought I loved my husband, but I found out that it was that   "Girl" that I really loved, and the man that didn't love me. So since I couldn't have the man that didn't love me I chose to stay with the man with that "Girl".   That way, that "Girl" and me could always be together.   I loved my husband but it was really that "Girl" that had me under her spell.   Weeks pasted by and I still was not happy.   I knew that I had to do something, but I just didn't know what, where or how, but this I did know, and that was, I wanted out.

My husband had left me to go out to purchase more of that "Girl".   I really wanted to be gone before he got back.   One of my girlfriends the man I was really in love with had introduced me to rode by the house.   Little to my surprise the man that I was in love with was sitting on the other side. He stated that he had heard of my troubles and he just wanted to see if I was ok.   My girlfriend told me at that time that I was a godmother of a new baby boy she had given birth to about 3 weeks prior to seeing me. She asked me if I wanted to come and spend some time with them.   I jumped in the car, and didn't look back, all I could think was this was my chance, because I just knew that my husband wouldn't have any idea that I would be at her house.

79

Soul Ties That Bind

Little to my surprise my husband hunted me down, and I was found. Of course he had been with that "Girl" because he had that sparkle in his eyes that she leaves when she engages herself. He was looking crazy in the eyes and I didn't want to cause any trouble in my girlfriend's home, so I left with him to keep peace. When I got in the car, it was a fight. He cursed me and called me all sorts of name. Once again he told me that I was stupid. We went through the same old thing whenever there was a fight. After awhile he stopped the car in the middle of the road and began hitting me with his fist, as I fought back, I said to myself surely I won't live through this, because my spirit, soul, and body was weakening from the fighting and blows. I was able to get out of the car, only by the grace of God, this I know now. I ran back to my girlfriend's home and begged her to please help me. I asked my girlfriend if I could call the police. I had the police to meet me at the home where we were staying. Out of all the times that we had fought, for some reason this time I really feared for my life. I kept feeling like this was going to be the end.

When the police arrived my husband had left the house and was on foot in the neighborhood somewhere. My girlfriend and her spouse followed me to the house to make sure there wouldn't be any trouble. My husband had thrown some of my material things out in the front yard. All I wanted was to get my things and leave, never to return. Little did I know the battle was just about to begin. I was torn between two opinions, one part of me wanted to stay there and make things better or at least try to work things out with my husband. The other part of me wanted to leave and forget I ever lived this kind of life, because surely it wasn't the way that I was brought up during my childhood, it was a life style that I chose to live.

When I told the police that I wanted to stay, he looked at me and said "Miss, you look like a very intelligent young lady and you're beautiful as well. If I let you go back into that house I

With Choices Come Consequences

will surely be back again. The officer assured me that if he left me there, he would be back in a matter of hours, not to help me out, but to identify my body because it would be badly beaten beyond recognition or identifying because of death. For some reason I felt this was God giving me a way out. The officer asked if I had some friends or relatives that I could stay with or go to for the night. I knew I couldn't go home to my mom and daddy because of what I did previous to this incident. My mother stated that she suspected that I was on something, now she knew for sure. She said these words that devastated me even more than everything that I had already experienced, " don't ride by my home to see if the bricks are standing and don't call my number to see if the phone is still connected." That hurt me worse than the blows I took from my husband.

The police officer asked me if my friend that was with me could at least let me stay the night with them. She asked her husband and he stated that it was all right, so the officer allowed me to get my car which was parked in the driveway, because it was in my name only. I left there with nothing but the clothes on my back and my vehicle. The strange thing about all of is that I didn't have any shoes on my feet. I don't have a clue has to what happened to them. The things thrown in the yard was not clothing. This is how the man with "that Girl" devastated me, when I talked about it in the beginning of my testimony.

At this point in my life, I didn't know which way to turn, but I knew one thing, I was on the road to recovery, from something, but I just didn't know what. I knew that God had answered my prayer from earlier that day that I wanted out. The longer I stayed with my friend that opened up their home to me, I knew one road of recovery I was on and that was no more of the man with that "Girl". I began another life living from pillar to post until I could get myself together.

After leaving that night, and believe me it was another long night that I had to endure, I went downtown with the advice of the police officer to take a warrant out on my husband and get him

Soul Ties That Bind

Off the streets.   The advice sounded good at the time because I felt like if he could get off the streets, that he would shake that "Girl" and get himself clean as I wanted to do.   So I proceeded down town to the police station to take out a warrant on him for assault on a female.

When I took out the warrant the magistrate told me that if I lifted the warrant that I would be locked up and confined to a cell.   That thought frightened me because I am afraid of being in very close places and being locked up.   Little did I know then that I was already locked up, bound by Satan and all his tactics in the natural all though the physical body was not incarcerated, I was incarcerated in the Spirit.   This is why Satan had to try his last attempt to take me out of this world, because he knew that his time with me was getting ready to come to an end.   I found out that they did arrest my husband for some previous warrants that had been taken out on him.   But little to my surprise I didn't know they would let him out the same night.   Within a matter of hours from me leaving the police station, he found where I was staying and because I wouldn't come back to him, took a bat out of anger and destroyed the one and only thing that I had left to call my own, yes that's right, my vehicle.   He smashed the windshield both front and back out, messed up the tires so that I was not able to drive it anywhere.   We called the police and again I had to take out another warrant on him for damage of private property.   Now everything I had was destroyed and I had nothing.

Tears ran down my face as I looked at my vehicle, broken hearted once again, and rejected, I didn't know which way to turn, so I just threw my hands up in the air and hollered to the top of my lungs.   Oh Lord, please forgive me for what I have done unto you, I can't take this way of life any more, please save me and show me the way.   Nothing happened at that moment, but I felt like I had some peace within and some strength to fight this battle. I wasn't able to sleep because I still had that "Girl" in my system, so I walked the floor all night long until finally I

With Choices Come Consequences

would pass out with exhaustion.   It has been a long day and night's journey, but I made that first step.

Sometimes the man that I was in love with would call me.   He finally came over after he found out what happened and the steps that I had made.   We would talk long hours in the night when everyone would settle in for the night.   He had a smooth way of calming me down when I was upset.   He seemed to have everything together and was such a gentleman.   He told me that if I were really serious about changing my life, now that he had me back he would never let me go.   I told him if he didn't mean what he was saying that I didn't want to have anything to do with him, because I had already been hurt enough.   He told not to worry about my family that he would talk to them.   He kept his promise and finally my mother and father called me.   They still wouldn't let me come home with fear that I would turn back again.   I had to prove to them that this time I was for real.   So they asked my friend and her husband if I could stay with them until after the court date.   They said that it was ok, so in exchange for my stay, my parents bought groceries to go into their home every week that I was there, I cleaned and kept the children. During this time I began to make up my mind that I was not going back.   I kept saying to myself, I'm free, of course the enemy tried to play games with me to make me think that I wasn't over the man or that "Girl", but every time he tested me from that point on I would past the test.   My husband would even come by every once in a while to beg me to please come back home.   He promised me he had given up that "Girl" forever, but I knew it was just to get me back in that trap again. He even sent the supplier to find me and beg me to come back. The supplier told me that they would move back in so we would not have to purchase that "Girl" anymore.   He even told me that my husband was about to lose his mind over me.   Sounded good but didn't work.   My mind was made up and I was not turning back. Weeks had passed, and one day I finally realized that I was going to make it.

My court date was finally coming up and my heart began to flutter, the enemy tried to put fear in me to make me think that I was not going to win this case. Well I prayed before going to court that day, and asked the Lord to go with me. My parents came with me to court. I had to prove to them that I was going through with this thing, before they would let me come home with them again.

Oh! By the way, I thought about this after the court date was over, there was a blizzard when this man came into my life, there was a severe thunderstorm the day we got married at the Justice of the Peace, because he didn't want to get married in the church. Lightening was striking the ground, and the day that I left him a hurricane, called Hugo came and tore up the city. So you see, there was nothing but storms in this relationship.

Now to end this testimony, let me give you some facts, by now I'm sure you know that "Girl" was cocaine, the man with that "Girl" was my husband, I went to court won the case, my husband went to prison and I started recovery. The man that I loved that didn't love me came into my life, and helped me to recover, I gave my life back to the Lord and He carried me one day at a time. I filed for a divorce from the man with that "Girl" only to find out that I was not legally married to him anyway, because he was still married to his first wife. They never divorced, and he didn't even know it.

I believe God allowed this to happen because there is a purpose that had to be fulfilled in my life for ministry and I am going to minister to those that has been rejected, beaten, battered, and broken as myself and looking for love in all the wrong places. This is why God let me know that I am a Mighty Woman Walking with Him. Because of the hell that I had to endure to get to where I am now.

I am now 42yrs. old, saved, sanctified, and filled with the Holy

84

With Choices Comes Consequences

Ghost, not only filled with Him but preaching and teaching his Word everywhere I go. I'm first ordained by God to preach the Gospel for such a time as this and to set the captives free. I have been placed here during this time to turn people from Satan's ways to God's ways. I am an ordained minister of the community and have been quite successful. Finally, I married the man that I loved that didn't love me. We have been married for 13 years. I have made two preaching CD's entitled, Armed and Dangerous, and From the Pit to the Palace. I'm currently in the process of writing the book, From the Pit to the Palace. I have a television program that is aired twice a week on the local cable channel in my hometown it is called, "Mighty Women Walking with God." This ministry reaches out to women who have been beaten, battered and broken, worn and torn by this world, women who are free in the physical sense but incarcerated in the Spirit.

This ministry touches those women in the church, and outside of the church. This ministry is a local and international ministry-reaching women of all walks of life. So please if this story of my life has caused you to see yourself, if you find yourself in anything similar to what I chose to do, please get out right now. Don't continue to waste your life, give your heart to God today.

After reading this book I do pray that you will not allow the enemy to keep you in bondage. There may be soul ties that are trying to keep you in that place you don't want to be, well, all you have to do is break those soul ties once and for all. Give your life to Jesus, He is the only one that can make you FREE INDEED.

Beaten, Battered & Broken To Mended
(B.B.B.T.M)
AN ABUSED WIFE

Lord help me make it through just one more day,
Help me be careful, watch what I do, and say,
Most of the time everything I say or even do is not right,
We end up arguing or fighting sometimes all night,
Please dear Lord, I hear his keys opening the door,
I am so tired I don't think I can take too much more,
I've been beaten down, battered, heart broken into,
Nights are so long I don't think I can make it through,
I cry dear Lord sometimes all through the night,
I'm so tired of the name-calling, tired of the fight,
God! Do You hear my prayer? Do You hear my plea?
I want to cry out just to say, "what about me?"
Lord! Will this nightmare ever come to an end?
Tonight I bear it and tomorrow I put on a grin.
I say to myself, you are nothing, you can't do it right,
That is all I've heard from him all my married life,
So then faith cometh by hearing, my esteem is so low,
Every time I get up, here comes another blow,
I found out Lord that I must continue to trust in You,
I read in my bible You are faithful, Your word is true,
You will never leave me, forsake me, no never,
I can count on You not just today Lord, but forever,
I've learned dear Lord in my everyday prayer to You,
You want me to pray for him inspite of what he do,
I realize that when I pray for him You fight for me,
This battle is not natural, one that you can see,

I'm not fighting flesh and blood, it's spiritual, it's sin,
God says "If you let Me fight for you, Satan can't win."
He says, you may be crying now but it won't be long,
I'll dry all your tears; your night will turn into dawn.
Yes Lord, right now I feel beaten, battered & broken into,
I know you promised in Your word to bring me through,
The reason I can tell this story so well,
There was a time I was held in that same cell,
My first husband would not change, and then he died,
Now I'm single, my minds made up in God I will abide,
God had plans for my life; He totally set me free,
He blessed me with a new husband that truly loves me,
Don't give up, wait on God, for He will come through,
I promise you, if He did it for me, He will do it for you.

Written By
---Evangelist Almetia Mack
DELIVERED AND MADE FREE BY JESUS
CHRIST!